Kübelwagen

A VISUAL HISTORY OF THE GERMAN ARMY'S MULTI-PURPOSE VEHICLES

and Schwimmwagen

by David Doyle

Published by
Ampersand Group, Inc.
A HobbyLink Japan company
235 NE 6th Ave., Suite B
Delray Beach, FL 33483-5543
561-266-9686 • 561-266-9786 Fax
www.ampersandpubco.com • www.hlj.com

Acknowledgements:
As always, the creating of this book required a great deal of help from a number of people. Key to bringing this book about were the members of the Kübel Korps USA club, among them Randy Smith, Dave Crompton, Rick Forys, Bob Graebe, Victor Vick, Bob Taylor, Barry Kemball-Cook, and David Lawhead. Also contributing immensely were Tom Kailbourn, John Adams-Graf, Kent Berg and Scott Taylor. As always, my dear wife Denise endured heat, rain, cold and thousands of miles to help me capture these images.

All unattributed photos are copyright of the author.

Cover: Iconic examples of Germany's light tactical vehicles and today highly sought collector vehicles, the Volkswagen Type 82 and its amphibious sibling, the Type 166 Schwimmwagen, pose together at the 2015 Kübel Korps reunion, a gathering for devotees of the types.

Rear cover: Unlike the Kübelwagen, the Schwimmwagen was a four-wheel drive vehicle, which combined with its amphibious capabilities resulted in the type being an able reconnaissance vehicle.

Title page: Designed by the legendary Ferdinand Porsche and produced by Volkswagen, the Kübelwagen served the same purpose in the German military as the Jeep served in the U.S. armed forces: a light-weight, versatile vehicle with good performance and mobility.

Table of Contents

A radio-equipped Kübelwagen drives through thick sand during the North Africa Campaign. The Conti Company developed a "balloon" type tire with improved performance on sand, but this car does not have those tires. (Patton Museum)

Introduction

Type 82 VW Kübelwagen

The vehicle that was to become the Type 82 Kübelwagen had its roots in the development of the Volkswagen "People's Car." Ferdinand Porsche, the well-known German designer, had been trying for years to get a manufacturer interested in a small car suitable for a family. In 1933, Adolf Hitler got involved, ordering the production of a basic vehicle capable of transporting two adults and three children. Prototypes of the car began appearing in 1936 and it was known as the "KdF-Wagen" (German: Kraft durch Freude–"strength through joy"). Although several thousand cars had been committed to holders of special savings books, none were actually delivered. One Type 1 Cabriolet was presented to Hitler on 20 April 1939.

With war clouds gathering over Europe, the efforts of the Volkswagen facility were turned to the production of military vehicles. In January 1938 work began in earnest on the vehicle that would come to be popularly known as the Kübelwagen.

The term Kübelwagen means "bucket car" and was actually applied to a variety of vehicles from a number of makers, but has come to be synonymous with the Volkswagen Type 82. Even under the skilled tutelage of Dr. Ferdinand Porsche, two years of work and testing were required before the Kübelwagen took its classic form.

A militarized version of the basic Volkswagen sedan was created, known as the Type 62. A much simpler version of the bodywork was conceived, composed entirely of stamped panels topped with a collapsible canvas top. It was to initially utilize the same chassis and drive train as the sedan, but modifications were necessary in order to improve its off-road performance. This included the addition of larger off-road tires, an increase in the width of the rear axle and raising the vehicle's ground clearance. After further testing, the new vehicle was ordered into production as the Type 82 VW Kübelwagen.

Its reliable, air-cooled engine and light weight made it both maneuverable and popular with the using troops. The vehicles were used from Africa to Russia, and proved successful in all theaters. Unlike the American Jeep, the Kübelwagen had only two-wheel drive, although four-wheel drive was experimented with on the Type 86 Kübelwagen. Various specialized versions of the Type 82 were built for use as radio vehicles, repair shops, ambulances and for intelligence work.

Interestingly, a vehicle combining the Kdf body and the Kübelwagen chassis was eventually produced. This was known as the Type 82E and was equipped very minimally for military use. The primary difference between the civilian car and the Type 82E was its markedly higher ground clearance. A four-wheel drive version was also developed, known as the Type 87.

In March 1943 the original 985 cc engine of the Kübelwagen was replaced with 1131 cc unit intended for use in the amphibious Schwimmwagen. At about the same time the instrument panel was redesigned and the fenders began to be welded rather than bolted on.

The Type 82E was the militarized version of the basic "People's Car" and was based on the chassis of the Type 82 Kübelwagen. Additional versions of the Volkswagen sedan were designed for wartime use. A transport van variant, an ambulance and a four-wheel drive cross-country car were among them. These variants were never as numerous as the ubiquitous Type 82 Kübelwagen. (PAS)

By April 1945, a total of 51,334 Kübelwagens of all types had been produced.

Schwimmwagen (Type 166)

Rivers and other bodies of water have formed natural defenses for thousands of years. Not surprisingly many attempts have been made to overcome that obstacle. One of the more successful devices for this purpose was the Volkswagen Type 166 Schwimmwagen.

Work began on this design, under Dr. Porsche's supervision, in July 1940. The development project was known as the Type 128. This early version of the concept had a longer wheelbase than the later production model. Its general layout was also different and it had the unique feature of selectable four-wheel drive. Thirty examples of the Type 128 were built in 1941 at the Wolfsburg Volkswagen Works and delivered to Wehrmacht and SS engineer units.

However it was not until February 1942 that the Schwimmwagen in its final form was approved for mass production. Dr. Porsche believed that the Type 128 was too unstable due to its size and he soon began on a new project known as the Type 166. The prototype of this version was tested in March of 1942, and production models began leaving the assembly line almost immediately. The Porsche Team produced the first 125 vehicles by hand at their facility in Stuttgart in June. These cars are sometimes known as "Vorserienschwimmwagen" or pre-series Schwimmwagen.

The early series bodies were completely handmade and the sides and bottom were welded from six pieces. The production series sides were stamped in one piece by the firm of Ambi-Budd. It also featured an improved 5-speed transmission and four-wheel drive. Water propulsion was by a manually retractable propeller. Like the Kübelwagen, Schwimmwagen's air-cooled engine was mounted in the rear of the body. By the end of the war over 14,000 of these machines had been delivered.

1940 Type 82 Kübelwagen

Here, the Type 82 prototype is on display in Berlin for the benefit of various Nazi dignitaries during the spring of 1939. The early-war camouflage pattern on the Kübelwagen can be seen. To left is the only civilian Volkswagen car to be delivered prior to the end of WWII: a Type 1 Cabriolet that was presented to Hitler as a gift. (NARA)

In this photo, the prototype is now on display on the streets of Berlin later that same day. It has garnered the attention of civilians and members of the SA as they get a closer look. (NARA)

The light weight of the prototype is demonstrated on the street as two men left the car to its right side tires. This was a deliberate part of the Type 82's design and was also a big part of the car's utility in the field. (NARA)

The canvas top has been folded back and four individuals have made themselves at home inside the Type 82. Details of the forward bodywork and spare tire are in evidence. (NARA)

A soldier adjusts a component in the engine compartment of a Kübelwagen at an automobile park. Next to the engine-compartment door is a Notek blackout taillight. A reflector is fastened to the lower left corner of the rear of the body. (NARA)

The driver of a Kübelwagen pauses to talk to an 88mm flak crew seated in an Sd.Kfz. 7 half-track prime mover in North Africa. The Kübelwagen has an FP (Feldpost: field post) license plate, number FP-14365, while the half-track bears Luftwaffe license plates. Side curtains are on the doors. (NARA)

At a site in the desert in North Africa, a Kübelwagen is parked among an array of vehicles. The rear of the body of the Kübelwagen is characteristic of vehicles up to body number 9,000, with a small shield or pan mounted under the center rear of the body. (NARA)

A German soldier, with an Italian to his rear, push a Kübelwagen on hard sand somewhere in North Africa. The canvas top has been painted in the same color as the wheels and body of the vehicle, but the canvas frames of the door curtains are unpainted. (NARA)

A disabled Kübelwagen is hitched to a cargo truck for towing to a repair facility in the El Agheila sector of Libya in January 1942. The car is painted in a yellow or sand color with a bit of camouflage in the form of a wavy, sprayed pattern in a dark color. (NARA)

A member of the Afrika Korps makes an adjustment to the oil-bath air cleaner in a Kübelwagen. To the right of his right hand are the distributor, the generator-drive pulley, and the oil filler cap. To the front of the engine is the fan shroud. (NARA)

Soldiers in a Kübelwagen pause during a troop movement in the desert while a fire rages in the distance. Balloon-type sand tires are installed on the wheels, and the tread pattern is visible on the spare tire. A Jerry can is stored in a rack above the left rear fender. (BA 784-0228-29A)

The driver of a Luftwaffe Kübelwagen looks to the rear as he tries to negotiate thick mud in Tunisia in 1943. The balloon tires that were effective on sandy terrain proved less suited for coping with mud. A horseshoe has been affixed to the left front fender. (BA 193-0031-10)

Seated in this Kübelwagen in southern Russia in 1943 are members of a Luftwaffe Kriegs-berichter Kompanie zur besonderen Verwendung (LW.KBK z.b.V: Luftwaffe war-corre-spondent company for special employment). (BA 635-3962-30A)

In a photo dated 21 June 1943 an MP in a Kübelwagen reads a document. Around the spare tire are various directional and informational signs, including one for "Feldgendarmerie" (military police). The tactical sign for military police is on the left fender. (BA 022-2926-07)

A Luftwaffe Kübelwagen equipped with balloon tires negotiates a rutted, muddy road. This vehicle has the intermediate-type rear pan, of wider design than the original pan and with two rectangular openings in it, produced from late 1942 to early 1943. (NARA)

Around the latter part of the 1944 Normandy Campaign, soldiers in and around a camouflage-painted, mud-spattered Kübelwagen survey a burning column of trucks on a highway. A railroad shipping stencil is visible on the driver's door. (BA 301-1960-24)

Allied troops made use of captured Kübelwagens whenever possible. This example with a crude identification star is in U.S. Army service in the North Africa or Mediterranean Theaters. Among graffiti on the body are "USA Arizona," "Berlin or Bust," and "Buzz." (NARA)

A group of G.I.s is riding in a captured Kübelwagen. An Allied recognition star is painted on the side to help prevent friendly-fire mishaps, but the vehicle still has a Wehrmacht license plate on the front. The sign appears to refer to Enna, Sicily. (NARA)

A G.I. touches-up a captured Kübelwagen with ample U.S.A. markings to announce its changed allegiance. The tires are heavy-duty directional treads, an unusual type for a Kübelwagen. They are more commonly fitted to Schwimmwagens and were designed for that purpose. Semperit, a company in Vienna, Austria, produced these. (NARA)

192455

A U.S. Army military policeman rests his arm on an improvised arm rest cut into the door of a Kübelwagen equipped with a front bumper rod (Vorderer Stossfänger) between the tow hooks: a feature installed on the production lines from late 1943 to early 1944. (NARA)

Apparently the Germans abandoned this Kübelwagen with a late-type spare tire carrier while it was undergoing painting and repairs. It has a fresh coat of light-colored paint, with overspray on the rear tire. Part of a rear license plate is visible: WH-925251. (NARA)

Top left: This Aberdeen Proving Ground photograph dated 20 June 1942 is the first of several of a captured Afrika Korps Kübelwagen. The tactical sign for a towed-artillery unit is on the left front fender. The rear wheels are missing and the vehicle is supported by a stand. **Top right:** The captured Kübelwagen is viewed from above. The dashboard is the early type produced until early 1943, while the steering wheel is the early type with thick spokes, made till mid-1942. To the rear of the front seats are four rifle holders. **Above left:** The underside of the Kübelwagen is viewed from a service pit, showing the front axle assembly and suspension, the front protection pan, and the bottom of the body. The front protection pan spanned from the front of the body to the rear of the front wheel wells. **Above right:** The engine of the captured Kübelwagen is displayed. From left to right are the air-intake hose, the air filter, the carburetor air-intake tube above the distributor, the carburetor, the generator pulley and regulator, and oil filler, with the fan shroud to the front of the compartment. (NARA, all)

A Kübelwagen assigned to the staff of the German 53rd corps (LIII Armee Korps - Korpsgruppe Bayerlein) stands by as Generalleutnant Fritz Bayerlein prepares to surrender on 19 April 1945. Bayerlein surrendered to General Robert Hasbrouck, commanding general of the 7th Armored Division, and ushered in the first of many mass surrenders by German troops that spring. Over 30,000 troops of the LIII Armee Korps were to pass into captivity. Like the vehicle on page 22, this one is equipped with heavy-duty directional tread tires. (NARA)

American soldiers are gathered around a Type 82 Kübelwagen with a G.I. behind the steering wheel. This vehicle dated from around the last month or two of Kübelwagen production and has the rare two-panel windshield. (NARA via Randy Smith)

WH-1636867

This beautifully preserved model-1941 Volkswagen Type 82 Kübelwagen exhibits a variety of early-production features. The short rear portion of the rear fenders is emblematic of very-early-production Kübelwagen. Other early-production features visible here include the early-type fuel filler and cap, the spotlight mounted on the right side of the windshield, and the absence of bumper rods. When built, this vehicle was fitted with 160mm or larger headlights, which have since been replaced with the later, small headlights shown here.

The removable side windows are installed on this Kübelwagen. The convertible top is retracted, showing the right side of the support framework. The bottom rear of the rear fender is approximately even with the bottom of the body adjacent to it. With body number 5000 the bottom rear of each rear fender would be lowered. Behind the front seats is a pedestal-mounted MG 34 machine gun.

Top left: A 1940-model Kübelwagen painted in Dunkelgrau (dark gray) is displayed in a museum setting. Owned and restored by Dave Crompton, this vehicle, body number 510, features a canvas convertible top of the early type, with two bows, one at the rear and one to the rear of the rear door. The support for the later top had three bows. **Top right:** The fuel filler neck and filler cap are to the right rear of the spare tire. The early type of filler included a flexible retainer to keep the cap from getting lost when removed from the filler. At body number 14001, a shorter and wider filler was introduced. **Above left:** Early Kübelwagens had a simple tow hook on each side of the front of the body; the right one is displayed here. Later, starting with body number 15371, redesigned tow hooks with a front bumper bar stretching between them were introduced to the Kübelwagen. **Above right:** Until early 1941-model Kübelwagens, a shovel was carried on the right front side of the body by means of a bracket for the shovel blade and a clamp for the handle. Late in the 1941 production run, the shovel and holders were moved to the left side of the body. (Rick Forys, all)

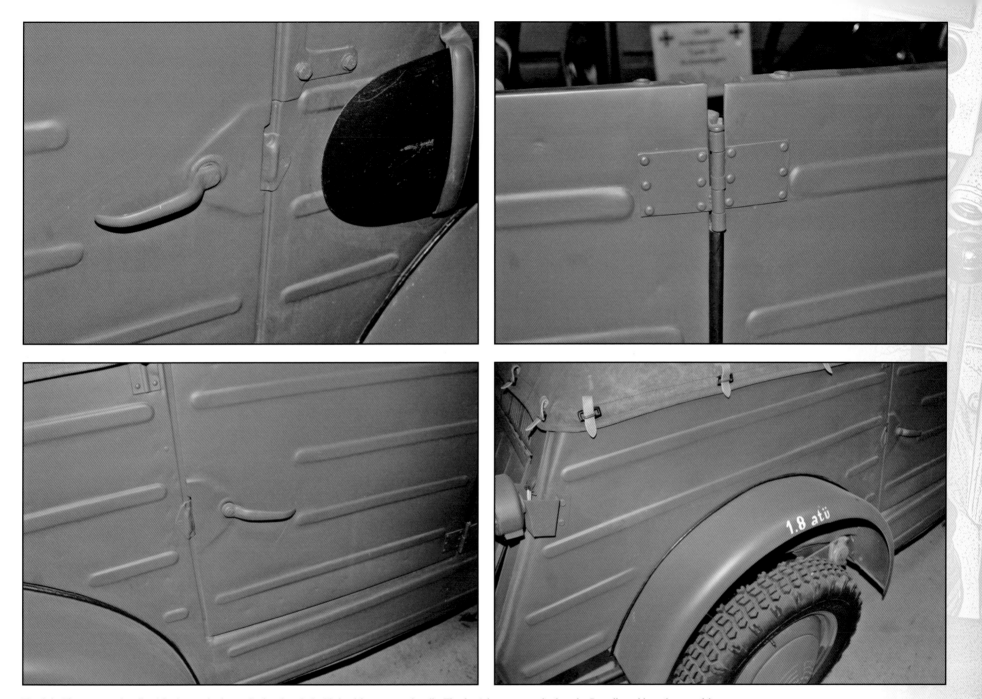

Top left: The operating handle of the front right door is displayed, with the blade of the stowed shovel to the right. On the exterior surface of the door where the handle joins it is an arrow-shaped raised section to provide clearance for the latch mechanism within. **Top right:** The upper hinge that serves both the front and rear right doors is shown. It and a lower hinge are attached to a vertical post inside the crew compartment, hidden from view here. Horizontal ribs were embossed into the door surfaces to give them extra rigidity. **Above left:** The right rear door of a 1940-model Kübelwagen is displayed, with the focus on the operating handle. The door's hinges are to the far right. Partially visible to the rear of the operating handle on the leading edge of the rear of the door opening is the strike plate. The two short ribs in the center of the door are indicative of 1940 production; from 1941 through 1945 these ribs were 10 cm longer for additional strength. **Above right:** The right rear body panel with its horizontal stiffening ribs, the right rear fender, and some of the hold-down straps and loops for the canvas top are in view. The recommended tire pressure for the rear tires, 1.8 atü, is painted on the edge of the rear fender. (Rick Forys, all)

Early-production Kübelwagens through body number 9000 in June 1942 had a narrow protection pan at the rear, visible here below the engine and fastened to the lower center of the rear of the body. A reflector hangs below the lower left rear corner of the body. (Rick Forys)

A restored Volkswagen Type 82 Kübelwagen is observed from the left rear. Above the right rear fender is a holder for a 20-liter Jerrycan liquid container fabricated from welded steel strips. The canvas top is rolled up and strapped on the rear of its support frame. The protection pan at the bottom rear of the body is the correct type for an early Kübelwagen, with four hex screws securing its top to the body and a small hole for a hand crank for the engine.

Top left: Several designs of treads can be observed in wartime photos of Kübelwagens. The tires on this preserved example are quite similar to one design of tread found on Kübelwagens in service in World War II. The valve stem is visible at the top of the wheel. **Top right:** From 1940 through March 1942 the Kübelwagen right rear quarter panel featured this type of taillight manufactured by Notek. The knob on the face of this aluminum-bodied lamp rotates a block inside the housing to darken the output during blackout conditions.

Above left: Early Kübelwagens had a ventilation grille for the engine compartment across the top rear of the body, above the engine-access lid. In 1943, because of dust and rain entering the engine compartment through this grille, an air duct cover was introduced that covered the entire grille. **Above right:** In the lower center of the engine-compartment access lid was a bowl-shaped indentation with a piece of steel rod riveted in place across the indentation. (Rick Forys, all)

Top left: The rear of the early-type rear protection pan is fastened with two hex screws to the body. This pan lacks the separate, overlaid plate at the top center that includes a small hole for the manual starting crank for the engine. Mounting holes for that plate are not present. **Top right:** At the lower left rear of the Kübelwagen is a reflector mounted on a bar that swivels at the top on a hinge. On early Kübelwagens, the two tailpipes were of a straight design; later, these were changed to a curved design that brought the pipes closer to the body, reducing damage in rough terrain. Above the tailpipe is the left rear tow hook. **Above left:** On the left rear of this early Kübelwagen is a Notek blackout taillight and, below it, a Wehrmacht registration plate. This type of taillight was used until body 29000, produced in late 1943. At that time, the engine compartment was modified, with two short ribs replacing the two left-most full-length reinforcing ribs, and the left taillight moved to the newly flattened position. **Above right:** The rear fenders on the Kübelwagen are rounded toward the outboard edge. A black weather strip is present between the fender and the side of the body. Visible between the rear of the tire and the rear of the fender is the rear end of the left tailpipe. (Rick Forys, all)

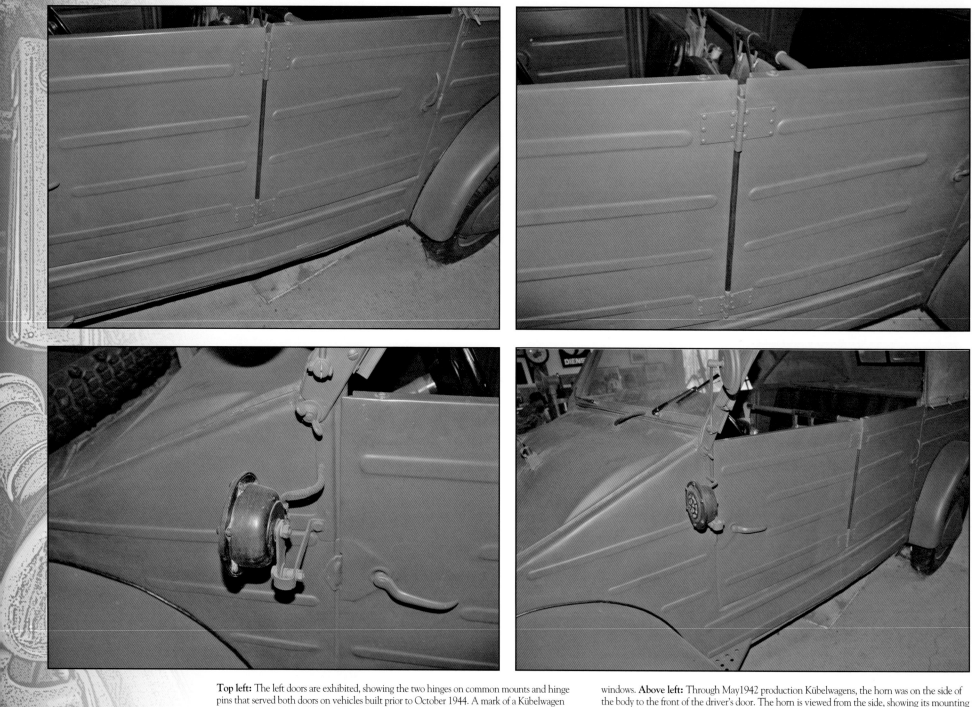

Top left: The left doors are exhibited, showing the two hinges on common mounts and hinge pins that served both doors on vehicles built prior to October 1944. A mark of a Kübelwagen that predates the May 1942 model is the absence of a socket for a jack on the side of the body below the bottom door hinge. **Top right:** The top hinge for the left doors is shown close-up. For each hinge, both doors share a common hinge pin, and the hinge leaf between the doors is attached to a column. The small holes atop the doors are sockets for mounting the detachable side windows. **Above left:** Through May 1942 production Kübelwagens, the horn was on the side of the body to the front of the driver's door. The horn is viewed from the side, showing its mounting bracket and electrical cable. Above the horn is the lower left side of the windshield frame. **Above right:** Several types of horns by different manufacturers were used on the Kübelwagen. The horn on this early-production example was manufactured by Westfälische Metallindustrie Lippstadt and was made of Bakelite, an early form of plastic made of synthetic materials. (Rick Forys, all)

Top left: An adjustable rear-view mirror is attached to the lower part of the left side of the windshield frame. Also on the side of the windshield frame is an early-type direction indicator, electrically operated, with a flip-up paddle to signal an intended turn, which was used until May 1942. **Top right:** At the lower corner of the joint between the front fenders and the side of the body is a triangular gusset or brace with ten lightening holes. The gusset for the left front fender is shown here. It has a turned-down outboard edge to add strength to the unit. **Above**

left: The front end of a 1940 model Kübelwagen sitting on jacks is observed from the left side. On the front fender is a service headlight with a blackout cover. Inboard of it is a Notek black-out headlight. Behind the front protection pan is the front axle assembly. **Above right:** The dome-type hubcap is embossed with the Volkswagen logo with a sprocket and stylized spinning swastika. This design of hubcap was used on prewar Volkswagen Beetles and according to some experts would not have been used on the Kübelwagen. (Rick Forys, all)

The spare tire was stored on a raised holder, not visible here, fitted with four arms called the spinne (spider), configured in an X shape. The pre-December 1942, pre-body 14001 featured long arms, with the two front arms almost reaching the front corners of the front deck. (Rick Forys)

WH-821940

Type 82 VW Kübelwagen	
Length	3.74 meters
Width	1.60 meters
Height	1.65 meters top up, 1.10 top down
Weight	1.15 tons loaded
Fuel capacity	40 liters
Maximum Speed	80 km/hr
Range, on road	400 km
Engine make	Volkswagen
Engine configuration	4-cylinder, horizontally opposed, air-cooled
Engine displacement	986 cc, later 1131 cc
Engine horsepower	23.5, later 25 @3000 RPM

Top right: The front left tow hook is displayed. The tow hooks are attached to the chassis frame and exit through openings in small metal plates riveted to the body. At the tip of each tow hook is a metal ring. **Above left:** In this view of the spare tire from the left side, the left rear arm of the early-type spider of the spare-tire holder or carrier is clearly visible. The spider arms are of hat-channel construction with a curved rather than flat top surface.

Above right: On the outboard side of the spare tire is the left rear arm of the spare-tire spider. The early-type spare tire carrier was semi-conical with long arms, while the late-model carrier introduced at around body number 15000 was more drum-shaped, with shorter arms. (Rick Forys, all)

Top left: The early-type fuel filler neck and cap are viewed from the front. A cap retainer with a black, flexible jacket is connected to the cap and the filler neck. To the rear of the tire is the windshield hold-down clamp; early Kübelwagens had only one such clamp. **Top right:** Another feature of the 1940-41 Kübelwagen was the spotlight on a flexible mount to the right side of the windshield. Spotlights were installed on these vehicles until late in the 1941 production schedule. To the rear of the spotlight is the right direction indicator. **Above left:** The pedestal for the spotlight is a curved tube with the bottom fastened to the side of the

body and a curved bracket fastened to the lower part of the right side of the windshield frame. A pintle mount is at the top of the pedestal. At the rear of the light is the push-pull light switch. **Above right:** The cab of the 1940 Kübelwagen was a model of simplicity. Separate seats were provided for the driver and front passenger. A dashboard positioned at the center of the cab is braced at the bottom by a curved tube. To each side of the instrument panel is a fuse box. Early production Kübelwagens utilized this style steering wheel, notable by having the three heavy spokes. (Rick Forys, all)

The engine-compartment lid is open on this 1941-model Kübelwagen, body number 5333, exposing to view the 23.5-horsepower, 985cc KdF engine and accessories. The early-type straight tailpipes are in evidence. A Jerrycan with a white cross signifying water is stowed on the fender. (Rick Forys)

Several early-production features are displayed in this view of the rear of a Kübelwagen, including the exposed ventilation grille above the engine-compartment lid, the narrow protection pan below the center of the body, and the presence of a service taillight. (Rick Forys)

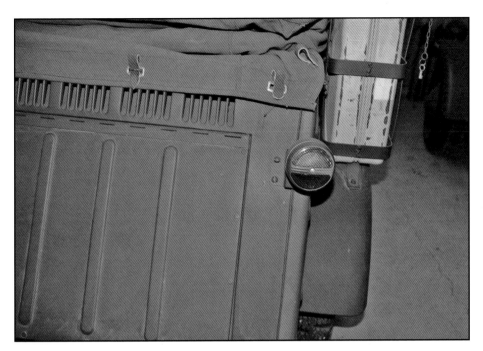

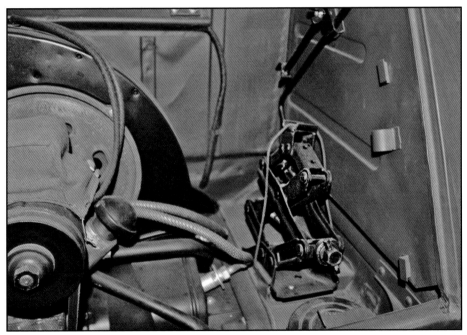

Top left: A standard service taillight was mounted on a bracket on the right rear of the body of Kübelwagens until Mach 1942 production. After this, the Notek blackout taillight on the left rear of the body served as the sole taillight component. **Top right:** The narrow rear protection pan is a key identification feature of early Kübelwagens and was present up to body number 9000 in June 1942. A separate plate at the top center of the protection pan included a small opening for admitting the engine manual-starter hand crank. **Above left:** Stowed in the right side of the engine compartment is the type of Scherenwagenbeber, or scissors jack, used by Kübelwagens through body 8500 in May 1942. To lift the car, it was placed at specific reinforced points under the body. Safety-wise, it left much to be desired. **Above right:** In a view of the engine compartment, at the center, to the rear of the pulley, are the generator and regulator with a canvas cover. To the left of the generator are the carburetor, air duct, oil-bath air filter and radio-suppressed distributor and special plug wires. To the front of the engine is the fan. (Rick Forys, all)

Top left: The black tubing to the left side of the engine compartment conducts air to the oil-bath air filter, center, which then sends purified air to the carburetor, far right. At the lower right is the distributor, to which are attached four braided ignition wires leading to spark plugs. **Top right:** In an overall view of the engine compartment of a 1941-model Kübelwagen, at the upper left is stored an oilcan. To the rear of the can is a fuse box. At the lower left are two retainer straps for a tool bag and an engine crank. To the far right is the scissors jack.

Above left: On the right rear corner of the model-1941 Kübelwagen body is the service tail light assembly, on a bracket attached to the body. The ventilation grille is visible on the rear of the body above the engine-compartment access lid. To the right is a Jerrycan. **Above right:** Details of the reinforcing ribs on the engine-compartment access lid and of the grille above the lid are displayed. The rear curtain of the canvas top is secured to loops attached to the body above the grille with russet leather straps. Two helmets are at the top. (Rick Forys, all)

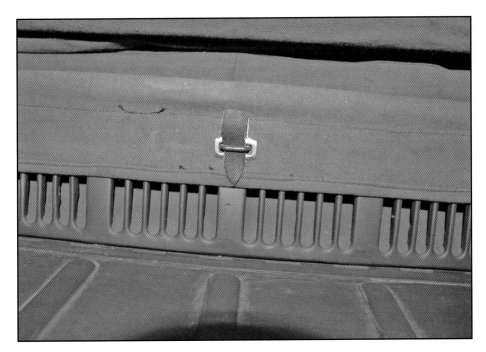

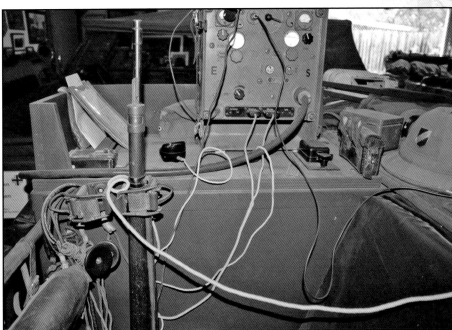

Top left: One of the leather straps that secures the rear curtain of the canvas top to a metal loop is shown in close detail. The canvas top could be completely removed from the vehicle, or it could be stored on the collapsible frame when not raised over the crew compartment. **Top right:** Some 3,326 examples of the Funkwagen, radio-equipped versions of the Kübelwagen, were produced in World War II. These cars carried various configurations of radio equipment. Mounted on the body of this example is a mount for a mast antenna. **Above left:** The antenna mount is viewed from the front. Depending on the vehicle and the equipment carried, the antenna mount could be found at various locations on either the right or the left side of the body. Some mounts were of lighter construction than this one. **Above right:** In this Funkwagen as viewed from the left side, the radio is on top of a special cabinet that occupies the right half of the rear of the cab, with seating remaining for one crewman at the lower left. A Mauser is stowed in the rifle holder to the left of center. (Rick Forys, all)

Top left: The front right corner of the rear compartment of the Funkwagen is observed. A leather case hangs from the cross-tube to the rear of the front seats. A radio headphone is stowed to the front of the Mauser. The radio operator's seat is to the bottom right. **Top right:** The radio installation in a Funkwagen based on a model-1941 Kübelwagen is viewed from the front right. The cabinet the camouflage-painted radio rests on is metal with a plywood top. A finger jointed semi-enclosure is attached to the plywood top. **Above left:** The front of the cab is viewed from the right. To the front of the dash to the right is the fuel tank. Two windshield-wiper motors are above the dash. At the center of the simple instrument panel is the speedometer. Between the seats is the transmission shift lever. **Above right:** Embossed on the dashboard to the upper left of the steering wheel column is the transmission shifting pattern. Kübelwagens were fitted with wooden grates on the floor of the cab featuring slats running front and rear on top with lateral slats on the bottom. (Rick Forys, all)

Top left: To the front of the driver's seat are the accelerator, clutch, and brake pedals. The central tunnel was not designed to accommodate a drive shaft, since the vehicle was rear-wheel drive, but was intended to add strength to the floor and to house control linkages. **Top right:** Between the front seats are the transmission shift lever and the parking brake lever. The parking brake is released when the lever is in the down position and is engaged by pulling up on the lever. **Above left:** The strike plate on the rear of the left rear door opening is shown. This hardware serves as a reinforced opening for the door latch to engage when the door is closed. The latch fits into the rectangular opening. The strike plate is fastened with three slotted screws. In 1943 these were attached by gas welding, and from 1944 they were spot-welded. **Above right:** One of the interior door handles and latch-mechanism housing are shown. To the left on the edge of the door is the latch. Above and below the handle are several of the horizontal ribs pressed into the surface of the door; seen from the inside, they are indented. (Rick Forys, all)

A restored Kübelwagen, body 11120, chassis 2-010605, owned by Bob Graebe is displayed with the convertible top deployed and with the detachable side windows installed. The direction indicators on brackets that stand off to the sides of the windshield were introduced in the first several months in 1942. The horn was moved to this position on the left side of the forward part of the body in late 1942, and the sockets in the side of the body below the doors also date to late 1942.

This restored Kübelwagen, body 21758, owned by David Lawhead, is an example from the early 1943 production run. The front and rear bumper rods, the front set of which is visible from this angle, were a key feature introduced in 1942. During part of the 1942 production, direction signals were included on curved arms extending from the sides of the windshield, and that feature is apparent here.

Top left: Brackets for stowing a shovel were mounted on the left front of the body from the 1942 to the early model-1944 Kübelwagen. Stenciled on the fender is the tire pressure, expressed in atmosphären überdruck, a measure of air pressure. **Top right:** Underneath the left front fender is a fender support and the electrical wire for the headlight mounted atop the fender. The electrical wire has a braided fabric jacket. The front and side edges of the fender are rolled for extra strength. **Above left:** The edge and the inner surface of the rear of the left fender are viewed from the side. Hex bolts and washers, barely discernible here, are used to fasten the fender to the side panel of the body. The triangular brace at the rear of the fender is in view. **Above right:** The 1943-model Kübelwagen is viewed from the left front with the driver's door open and the top folded down. Mounted between the left headlight assembly and the spare tire is a Notek blackout headlight. To the front of the headlight is the horn.

Top left: The late-type direction indicator is mounted on tubular supports with two attachment points to the body. The exposed cable to the left powered the windshield wipers; this cable was no longer routed there after body number body number 25000 around July 1943. **Top right:** The driver's rear-view mirror is mounted on a stub on the side of the support for the left direction indicator. On top of the windshield frame are two studs for attaching the frame that supports the canvas top. The left stud is in view here. **Above left:**

The driver's door is open, displaying the design of its front edge, into which is recessed the door-latch mechanism. Two large, slotted screws secure the latch in position. The interior operating handle of the door also is visible. **Above right:** In a view looking downward, the open driver's door is to the lower right, and the left side of the driver's seat is in view. Below the seat cushion, part of the supporting frame of the seat can be discerned. The front seats were adjustable.

The steering wheel on this 1943-model Kübelwagen is the late type; with a Bakelite rim, metal spokes, and the horn button on the hub. The instrument panel is the early pattern, used until early 1943. The rectangular shapes to each side of the instrument panel are fuse boxes. At the bottom of the windshield frame are the two windshield-wiper motors. Exposed to the right side of the dash is the fuel tank.

Clamped to the center of the tubular rail to the rear of the front seats is a clip for stowing four rifles in a vertical position. Straddling the clip and also clamped to the tubular rail is a stowage rack for an MG 34 machine gun. At the bottom is the wooden floor grating.

To the rear of the rear seats, above the engine compartment, is a lid for a stowage compartment. On the lid is a machine-gun tripod secured to clamp-type brackets. The vertical tube to the rear of the tripod is a pedestal mount for an MG 34 machine gun.

On very early Kübelwagens, the rears of the rear fenders were short, ending at the level of the bottom of the rear of the body. From about body number 5001, the rears of the fenders were extended lower, as seen here, with a triangular brace at the rear.

Top left: The bracket for the left side of the support frame for the convertible top is viewed close-up. For extra strength, the bracket extends a few inches down the side of the body, and a tie-down loop of bent wire is welded to the bracket. Another loop is to the right. **Top right:** Early Kübelwagens had straight tailpipes, but from body number 9001 on they had curved tailpipes such as this one. There was an exhaust, muffler, and tailpipe assembly on each side of the vehicle; this one is on the left side. **Above left:** Throughout most of the production run of the Kübelwagen, a box-shaped Notek blackout taillight was mounted on the upper left rear of the body. One such unit is shown here, with its mounting bracket and clips to hold the cover in place. **Above right:** The Notek blackout taillight, as viewed from the rear, has a hinged flap. In non-blackout conditions, the flap was raised, as shown here, to expose the red taillight (left) and orange brake light, right. The flap was lowered in blackout conditions.

Top left: The lower left of the rear of a Kübelwagen is viewed close-up. Directly below the registration plate is a swiveling latch for holding the engine-compartment lid shut. Below it is the left rear tow hook and bumper-rod support. **Top right:** A round taillight assembly was on the upper right rear of the body until body number 9000 in the 1942 production run. At the top corner of the body above the engine-compartment lid is a cover fitted over the ventilation grille. **Above left:** The standard taillight is viewed from the rear. Below the light is the electrical cable for the light, with a braided fabric jacket. The light features an orange brake light over a red running light lens, and the cover is fastened to the light housing with a single screw in the center. **Above right:** The taillight assembly is viewed from the right side, also showing its mounting bracket, which straddles the right rear corner of the body. Two large, slotted, round-headed screws that hold the right side of the bracket to the body are in view.

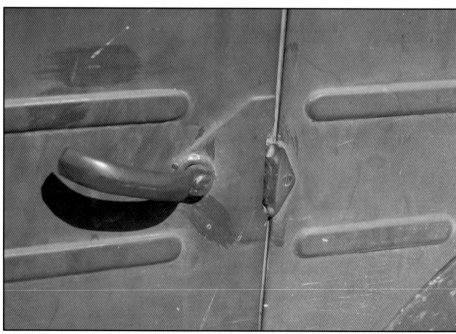

Top left: On the right side of the body of this Kübelwagen is a rack for a 20-liter "Jerrycan" liquid container, fashioned from welded steel strips. Such racks occasionally were located at this position or above the front fenders as a field modification. **Top right:** The rack for the Jerrycan is fitted with two legs made of steel strips, attached to the top of the rear fender for extra strength. The Jerrycan simply rested in the rack, without any kind of an upper retainer. The curved right tailpipe is visible. **Above left:** Jerrycans were fabricated from pressed steel.

The spout and cap are to the upper front of the can from this angle, and three handles are below the spout. Different types of cans were marked for carrying water, wasser, or, here, fuel, or kraftstoff. **Above right:** At the point where the exterior operating handle of the front right door is, there is a slight swelling in the surface of the door, with a pointed shape facing forward, to provide clearance for the operating mechanism within the door.

A bent, tubular assembly running across the front of the cab of the Kübelwagen served to support the bottom of the instrument panel and dashboard, thus eliminating the need to extend the dashboard across the entire width of the cab.

Top left: Embossed in raised figures on the upper left of the dashboard is a diagram showing the transmission-shifting pattern. Above the speedometer is the Volkswagen logo. The large black switch to the lower left of the speedometer is the choke control. **Top right:** To the right of the dashboard is the fuel tank, with a metal strap support visible. Underneath the tank but not visible here is a fuel cock. The fuel tank held approximately 10½ U.S. gallons. To the right is the inside of the front right door. **Above left:** The interior operating handle of the right rear door of a Kübelwagen is displayed. The horizontal ribs that served to stiffen the skin of the body were stamped into the panels and appear as recesses in the skin from the inside of the vehicle. **Above right:** The late-type fuel filler and cap were introduced with body number 14001, in December 1942. The filler was lower and wider in diameter than the early-type filler, and the late-type filler cap was larger than diameter than the early type.

A 1943-model Kübelwagen is observed from the front right. To the rear of the spare tire is the late-type fuel filler and cap. Extending between the two front tow hooks is the front bumper rod, a feature introduced with the 1943-model Kübelwagen.

Top left: The right direction indicator is mounted on a tubular support with two attachment points to the body, but, unlike the support for the left direction indicator, the right support lacked a stub on the side for mounting a rear-view mirror. **Top right:** The right direction indicator is viewed from the front. The curved bottom of the tubular support forms the lower attachment point to the vehicle's body, while the upper attachment point is on the inboard side of a tube welded to the support. **Above left:** The spare tire is a modern Wesa Gelände, size 5.25-16. The double-dome hubcap with the Volkswagen logo is secured to the wheel rim with mounting brackets. These hubcaps and mounting brackets were discontinued after mid-1943. **Above right:** Extending across the front of the body of the Kübelwagen is the front bumper rod. This feature was introduced during 1943 production. A towrope fitted with eyes on the ends is secured to the front tow hooks. To the right is the horn.

Various features of the front end of a of 1943 Kübelwagen, body 21758, are displayed. At the top is the exposed windshield-wiper hose, present until late in the production of Kübelwagens. The windshield clamps are to the rear of the spare tire, the hubcap on which is the double-dome type with the Volkswagen logo at the center. At the front of the left bumper is the horn; Hella made this type. Below the bumper rod is the front protection pan, with three vertical ribs stamped on it.

The spare-tire holder was a separate assembly attached to the front deck of the body. To the rear of the spare tire are two windshield hold-down clamps; these two clamps replaced the 1940 configuration of one clamp at the center of the deck.

Top left: The late-type fuel filler and cap and the right windshield hold-down clamp are seen from the front. The filler formed a tube, slightly wider at the bottom than at the top, with a sloping extension to the rear of it, seen here and in preceding photos. **Top right:** The left windshield hold-down clamp is at the center of the photo, with part of the left windshield clamp to the top left. These clamps were mounted on a raised bracket and included a steel clip and a rubber bumper, partially hidden here by the clip. **Above left:** Throughout its production history the Kübelwagen had a slight bulge across the rear portion of the front deck of the body, and that feature is visible here. The windshield hold-down clips were welded to the forward part of that bulge. **Above right:** The flexible electrical cord with a braided fabric jacket is routed up through a fitting attached to the front deck of the body. After entering the bottom of the windshield frame, separate electrical wires are routed to the two windshield wipers.

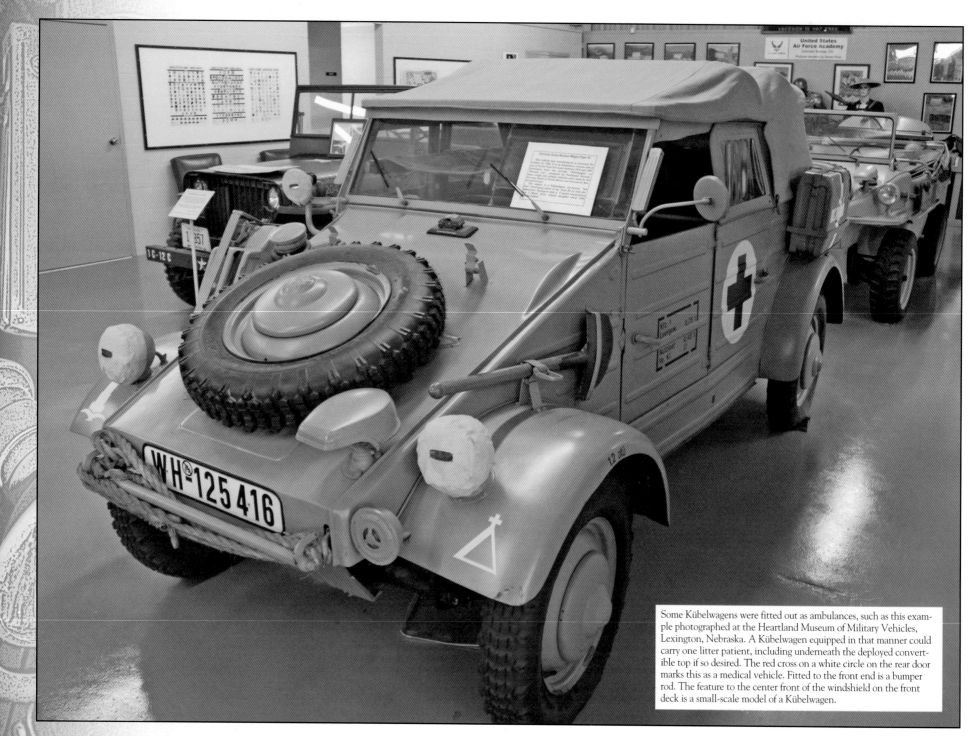

Some Kübelwagens were fitted out as ambulances, such as this example photographed at the Heartland Museum of Military Vehicles, Lexington, Nebraska. A Kübelwagen equipped in that manner could carry one litter patient, including underneath the deployed convertible top if so desired. The red cross on a white circle on the rear door marks this as a medical vehicle. Fitted to the front end is a bumper rod. The feature to the center front of the windshield on the front deck is a small-scale model of a Kübelwagen.

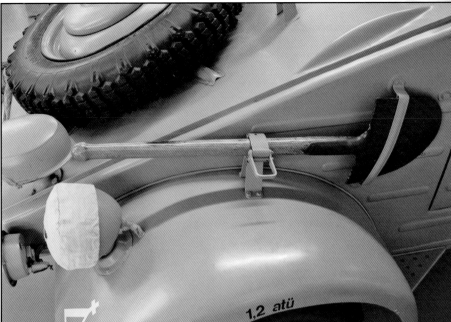

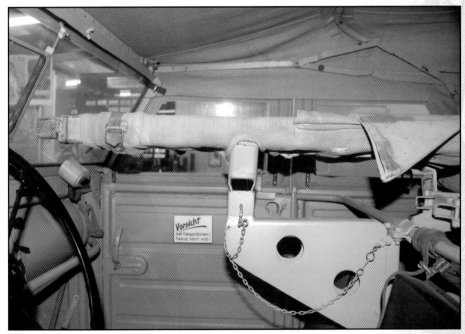

Top left: The spare tire has a double-dome hubcap with VW logo. The service headlights are equipped with blackout covers with a horizontal slot to emit a small amount of light. Gone is the exposed cable for the windshield washers, omitted from body number 25001. **Top right:** The blackout cover on the left service headlight is observed from the left side. Inboard of the headlight is the Notek blackout headlight, and to the front of the service headlight is the horn. A close-up view is also provided of the shovel bracket and clamp-type holder. **Above**

left: During the 1943 production run, from body number 25001, the original instrument panel was replaced with a new design with a smaller speedometer (not visible from this angle) and rearranged controls. The dark object at the top of the panel is the fuse box. **Above right:** Inside this Kübelwagen are provisions for transporting a litter patient. To the right of the driver's seat is the left front litter holder. The sign on the door reads, "Caution: during conversations the enemy listens!" Part of the frame supporting the canvas top is visible.

Visible from this angle are the left and right front litter holders. The left front holder is supported by a post and by an attachment to the rail to the rear of the front seats. The right front holder is fastened to the column between the front and rear doors.

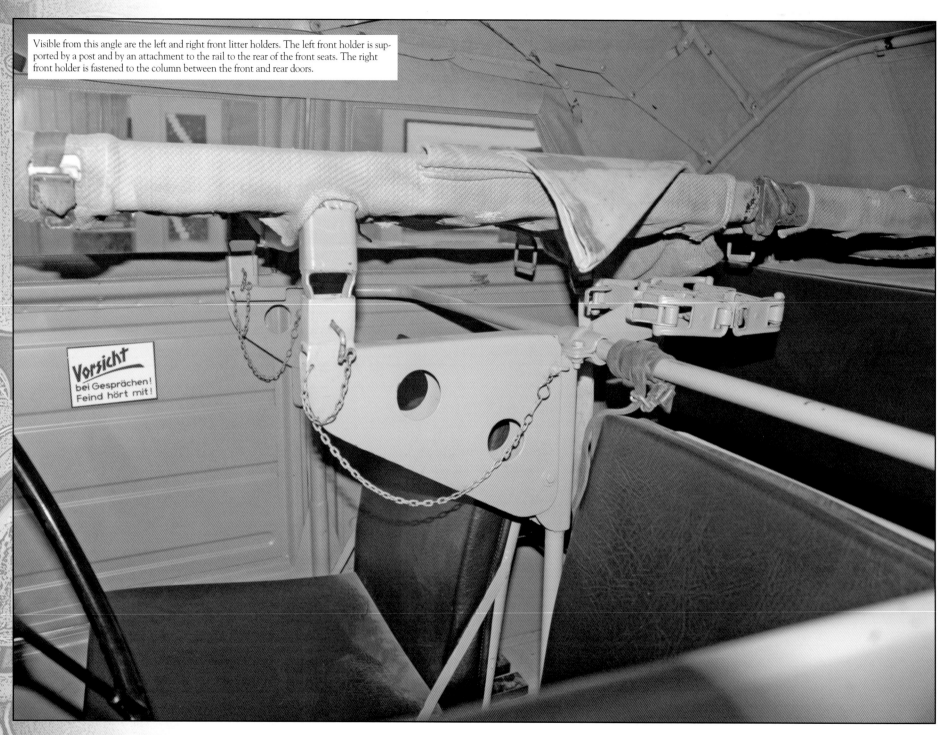

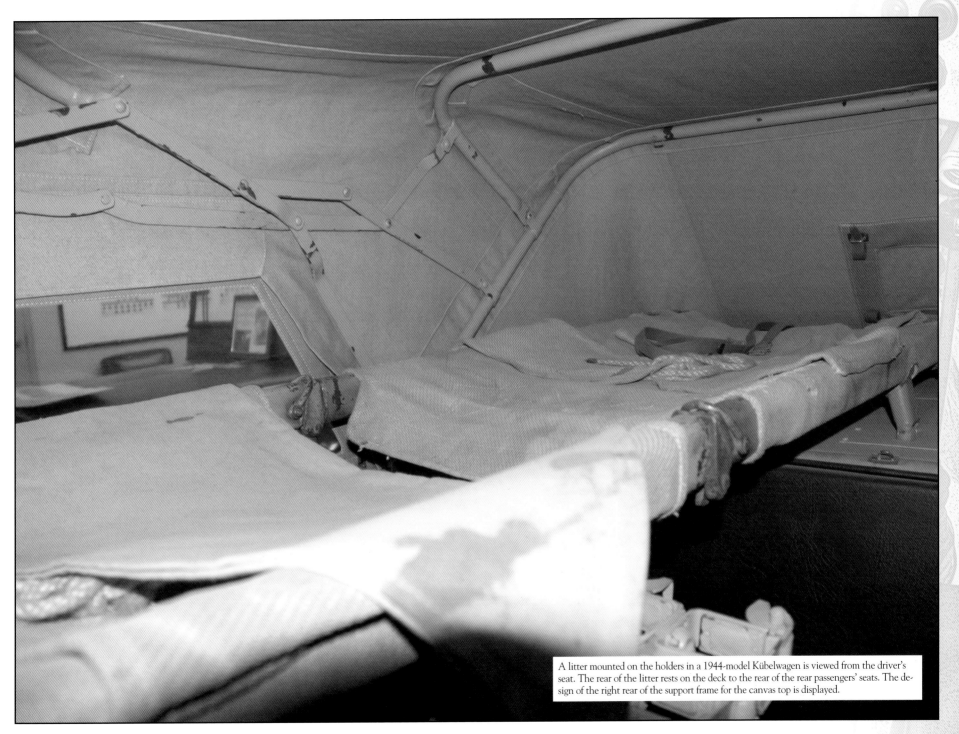

A litter mounted on the holders in a 1944-model Kübelwagen is viewed from the driver's seat. The rear of the litter rests on the deck to the rear of the rear passengers' seats. The design of the right rear of the support frame for the canvas top is displayed.

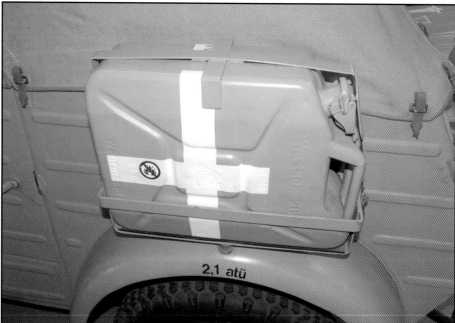

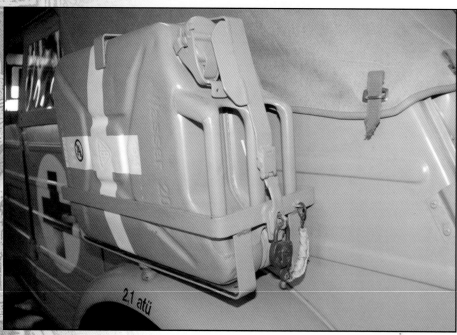

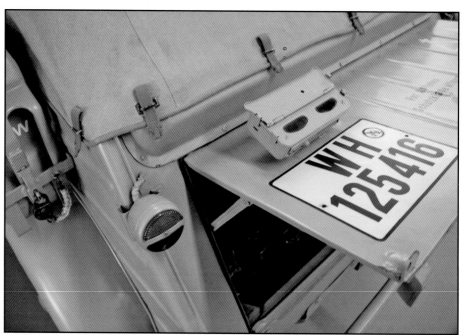

Top left: The handle on the left rear door is the late type, which was a flatter and wider design than the early, cylindrical type. To the lower left is the left jack socket, a feature introduced with body number 8501. To the top center is a hold-down strap for the canvas top.
Top right: This Kübelwagen is equipped with an unusual liquid-container holder over the left rear fender. The Jerrycan is marked with a white cross, a device that indicated that the contents were water rather than fuel. "Wasser" (water) also is stamped on the can. **Above**

left: The liquid-container holder has an upper hold-down element that is padlocked at the lower rear. To the top right is the grille cover. **Above right:** The engine-compartment lid is of the final design, introduced in late 1943-model vehicles at body number 29001, with two very short reinforcing ribs stamped into the upper left of the lid, hidden here by the Notek blackout taillight, which had been relocated here. The taillight to the left was not present on the Kübelwagen as it came from the factory and is apparently a postwar modification.

Top left: In a view of the engine compartment, the unit with the red label at the center is the oil-bath air filter. To the far right, connected to the air duct from the air filter, is the carburetor. To the lower left is the jack, above which is the air-intake hose. **Top right:** Stowed on clamps and holders on the inside of the engine-compartment lid are a hand-operated tire pump and a crank for manually starting the engine. Not all Kübelwagens were outfitted with these tools on the interior of the engine-compartment lid. **Above left:** Attached to the top pulley is the generator, with the regulator on top of it. To the side of the generator is the red oil-filler cap. To the front of the engine is the fan housing. The green canister above the oil filler contained ether for cold-starting the engine. **Above right:** Although service taillight assemblies, including the right one shown here, are mounted on both sides of the rear of this 1944-model Kübelwagen, these taillights were discontinued following body number 9000 during production of the 1942 model.

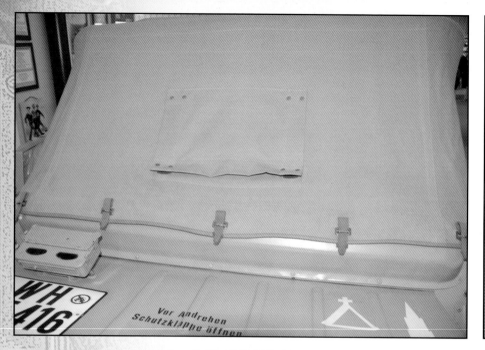

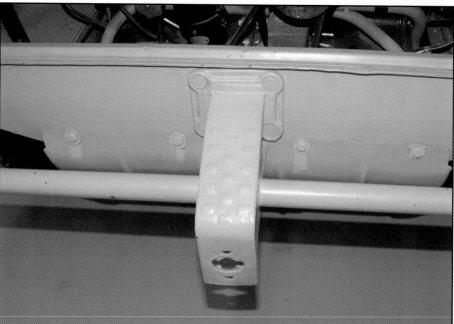

Top left: The rear of the canvas top, its center window flap, and tie-down straps are in view. The bottom of the canvas top overlaps the grille cover. On the engine-compartment lid, the late-model positions of the registration plate and blackout taillight are displayed. **Top right:** In a view of the lower rear of the 1944-model Kübelwagen, the support bracket/step at the center of the rear bumper rod is at the center. The hole in the rear of the bracket is for the hand-starting crank for the engine. Non-slip nubs are on the top of the bracket/step. **Above**

left: This view of the lower right rear of the vehicle reveals details of the right muffler and tail pipe at the center. The exhaust line from the engine is to the left, and the tailpipe is to the right. To the far left is the right side of the late-type rear lower protection pan. **Above right:** The operating handle of the right rear door is portrayed close-up. The arrow-shaped bulge where the handle is attached to the door is apparent. Fastened to the edge of the door opening to the left or rear of that bulge is the strike plate, which engages the door latch.

Top left: A spotlight of the type shown here was factory-mounted on the Kübelwagen up to late 1941, after which it was discontinued. Although this spotlight apparently was retrofitted on this 1944-model Kübelwagen, the photo demonstrates its mode of mounting. **Above left:** Above the support bracket for the spotlight and attached directly to the right side of the windshield frame is an early-model right direction indicator. Direction indicators were eliminated from the Kübelwagen after body number 15655 in February 1943. **Right:** The early-type right direction indicator and the spotlight, both of which were not standard on 1944-model Kübelwagen as depicted here, are viewed from the front. The spotlight is fitted with a fabric blackout cover to limit the amount of light emitted from the unit. The direction indicator was electrically operated and featured a swiveling indicator that remained inside a housing when not being operated.

Over the front right fender of this Kübelwagen is a liquid-container holder of a completely different design than the one above the rear left fender. A retainer made of strap steel and two hinges serves to keep the Jerrycan firmly in the holder.

This Kübelwagen, body number 48021, owned by Victor Vick, represents a late-production, 1944-model vehicle. The bumper rods present on Kübelwagens from 1942 to September 1944 had been discontinued, but front bumper rods have been applied to this vehicle. Lacking the proper type of tow hooks used with the bumper rods, the rod has been welded to the bottom of the tow hooks. Stenciled on the side of the driver's door is weight and vehicle-class information.

Top left: The left side of the improvised front bumper rod is viewed close-up. The horn next to the hook is the type produced by Hella. The front arms of the late-type spare tire carrier are farther back from the front corners of the front deck than on the early-type carrier. **Top right:** The rear of the original Hella horn was fabricated from Bakelite, and this example has a brownish-red color. The rear of the horn is fastened to a bracket attached to the body. The service headlight and the Notek headlight and their mountings are viewed from the side.

Above left: The steering wheel is the late type, introduced in mid-1942, with a Bakelite wheel and thin metal spokes. This replaced the early, all-Bakelite wheel. The instrument panel is the early type, used up to body number 25000 in the early-1943 production run. **Above right:** Details of the driver's seat, the instrument panel, the fuel tank to the far right, the windshield-wiper motors, transmission shift lever, parking brake lever, central tunnel, and brake, clutch, and accelerator pedals are viewed from the front passenger's seat.

Top left: The rear part of the support frame for the convertible top is in view, showing the center bow and the rear bow. The deck behind the rear seat was a stowage-box cover; this is the late type, introduced at body number 29001, with only one long rib on its right half. **Top right:** The left rear part of the convertible-top frame is observed. The frame pivots on the mounting to the front of the rear seat back. Two rectangular clear plastic windows are in the rear of the canvas top. Three long ribs are on the left half of the stowage-box cover. **Above**

left: In a view of the lower rear corner of the side of the body, the late-style curved tailpipe and, immediately to the rear of it, the reflector is visible. Whereas a front bumper rod has been installed on this vehicle, no effort was made to place a rear bumper rod on it. **Above right:** The design of the rear corner of the Kübelwagen body is observed from the left side. Above the engine-access lid on the rear of the body is the grille cover. Visible in profile on the left side of the lid is the Notek blackout taillight, relocated here late in production.

On very-late-production Kübelwagen bodies, the two vertical ribs on the left side of the engine-access lid were shortened, making for a flat surface to which the registration plate was directly applied. Also at that time, the blackout taillight was relocated to the lid.

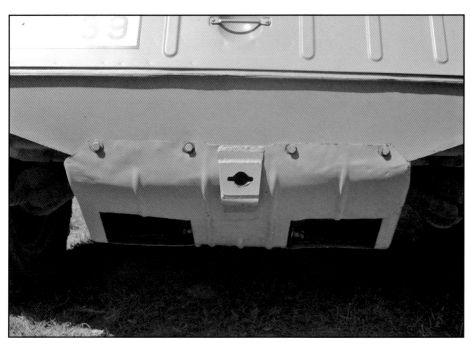

Top left: The redesigned engine-access lid was introduced with body number 29001 late in 1943-model production. The blackout taillight has the lid in the raised position, exposing the two oblong, red non-blackout lenses and masking the blackout lenses at the top. **Top right:** At each lower corner of the engine-access lid is a swiveling-type fitting for securing the lid in the closed position. Below the fitting is the left rear tow hook. Below and to the left of the tow hook is the reflector, mounted on a metal strip that is hinged at the top. **Above left:** A rear protection pan that was wider than the early type was introduced with body number 9001, with a fitting for an engine hand crank at the upper center. **Above right:** Although a single taillight on the right rear of the body was a feature of early Kübelwagens, this late example has a taillight mounted. To the left of the tow hook are two of the hex bolts referred to in the preceding photo as a late-production feature. On each side of the sill above the top of the protection pan are two hex bolts, a late-production feature.

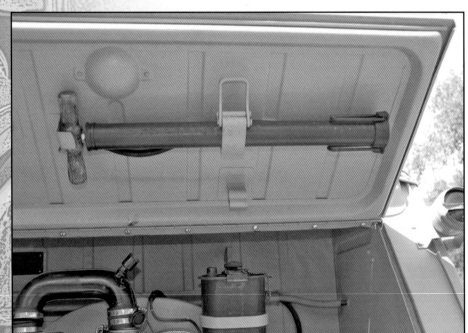

Top left: The top of the engine-compartment access lid is connected to the upper rear of the body with a piano hinge. Toward the lower center of the lid is a bowl-shaped recess with a grab handle welded on each side of the recess. Details of the canvas top are portrayed. **Top right:** At the center of this view of the left half of the engine compartment of a late Kübelwagen is the oil-bath filter, to the right of which is the carburetor. Stowed in brackets to the left is the insertable-type jack. To the upper left is the hold-open arm for the lid. **Above left:**

Stowed on a bracket and a clamp on the inside of the engine-access lid is a tire pump. The dark green, flask-shaped object below the pump is a container for ether for starting the engine in extreme cold conditions. The dome above the pump is for the grab handle. **Above right:** Secured with a strap and a clamp-type buckle on the floor of the right side of the engine compartment is a wooden toolbox. The box is marked "Werkzeugkasten Typ 82" (Toolbox Type 82) and with the initials for Liebstandarte SS Adolf Hitler.

Top left: The vehicle is viewed from the right front, showing the right service headlight, the front bumper rod, the spare tire, the fuel filler and cap, and the right fender. Marked on the right fender is the insignia of 1st SS-Panzer Division Liebstandarte SS Adolf Hitler.
Top right: The same area in the preceding photo is observed closer. The spider arms of the spare-tire carrier are the late type, noticeably shorter than those on early-production Kübelwagen. These shorter arms were introduced around body number 15000 in early 1943.

Above left: The rod across the front of later-production Kübelwagens offered scant protection from collisions. Instead, it served primarily as a lifting bar to aid extricating mired vehicles. **Above right:** The front bumper rod on this 1945-model Kübelwagen is apparently a postwar addition, since that feature had been discontinued on new-production vehicles by the end of 1944, at or around body number 29001. This bumper rod has been simply welded to the bottoms of the tow hooks.

Top left: On some Kübelwagens, several designs of machine gun mounts were installed to the front of the front passenger's position to provide the crew with a powerful forward defensive capability. This example has two triangular bases on each side of the fuel filler. **Top right:** A cross-tube with a locking lever passes through the two triangular base plates; welded to the cross-tube is a gusseted tube that supports a pintle mount for the machine gun. This type of mount was typically found on reconnaissance vehicles termed Volkswagen-Züge. **Above left:** The machine gun mount is observed from the left side. The pintle that holds the gun swivels on the rear of the tubular arm. **Above right:** An MG 34 7.92mm machine gun is installed on the pintle mount. A bipod is fitted near the muzzle for operation away from the vehicle. A drum magazine is attached to the receiver. The MG 34 had an incredible rate of fire: up to 900 rounds per minute. To the right is a Panzerfaust, a recoilless antitank weapon with a disposable tube from which a high explosive antitank (HEAT) projectile was launched.

This beautifully restored Type 82 Kübelwagen, body number 51639, owned by Scott Hayes was produced 21 January 1945 and represents a vehicle built near the end of that vehicle's production run. Some of the late-production attributes visible in this photo include the so-called half hinges on the doors, the elimination of the spade mountings from the left side of the front of the body (as well as the right side), and the omission of the cross-bar from the front tow hooks. (Randy Smith)

Left: A perforated gusset helps to stabilize and reinforce the bottom of the front fender. Also in view are the left headlight and its power cable, the horn with its dark brown Bakelite case, and the Notek blackout headlight. **Top right:** The front license number was painted inside a raised border on the front of the body. Superimposed over the dash on this reproduction license number is a reddish colored stamp. Note that the ends of the legs of the spare-tire spider are open. **Above right:** The windshield hold-down latches (the left one is shown) on the Kübelwagen from 1944 to the end of production were a simplified type, without the rubber bumper found on earlier versions of the devices. On the lower part of the windshield frame is the single windshield-wiper motor. (Randy Smith, all)

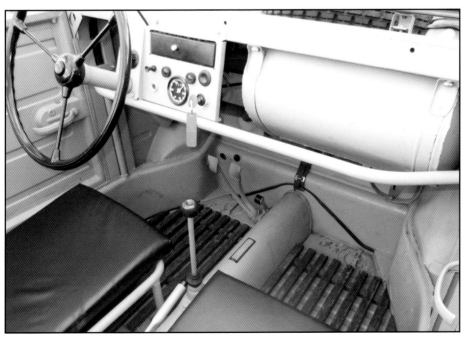

Top left: The left side of the front suspension is viewed from the front left corner of the vehicle, showing the left ends of the axles. Attached to the ends of the axles are support arms. Also visible is the inner face of the wheel and elements of the steering mechanism. **Top right:** The interior of the very late-production Kübelwagen is seen from above the engine compartment, providing an idea of the construction of the rear of the two front seats. At the center of the cross-bar above the seats is a holder for four rifles. **Above left:** The late Kübelwagen featured a simplified, Schwimmwagen-style dashboard, with a lateral tubular support for the steering wheel and the instrument panel. The fuel tank is visible to the right of the instrument panel. Above the tunnel are the transmission shift lever and the hand-brake lever. The steering wheel is the late design, with three thin metal spokes. **Above right:** Affixed to the top of the tunnel of this very-late Type 82 Kübelwagen, as seen from the left side, is a small plate bearing what is called the "tunnel number," which in this case is 2-049076. The button with the letter L on it is the choke control. (Randy Smith, all)

The dark-colored rectangular feature at the top of the instrument panel is the fuse box. On the dash below the instrument panel and above the front end of the tunnel is a recess in which a Jerrycan is stored. According to some sources, a crew kit sometimes was stored in that recess. (Randy Smith)

Top left: The battery box is below the left side of the rear seat of the Kübelwagen. It was of wooden construction. To the right is the rear seat, folded forward, showing the springs below the upholstery. To the upper left is the rear seat back. **Top right:** Stamped into the sill on the left side of the driver's seat is the Kübelwagen's body number, 51639. **Above left:** The reproduction painted-on license plate and the Nachtmarschgerät (night-march device) blackout taillight are viewed close-up. At the bottom corner of the engine-compartment lid is a swiveling latch. **Above right:** The Notek taillight on a very late-production Kübelwagen is viewed from below, with the painted-on license plate at the bottom of the photo. The flap of the taillight is in the raised position, allowing the non-blackout lights at the bottom of the unit to show. When the flap was lowered, the blackout lights at the top of the unit were exposed. Here, on the rear face of the unit, the left light is a taillight and the right one is a brake light. (Randy Smith, all)

From approximately October 1943, the license plates were painted on the lower left corner of the engine-compartment lid of the Kübelwagen. Above the rear license plate is a blackout taillight. (Randy Smith)

The engine compartment of the late-production Type 82 Kübelwagen had a distinctive appearance, including the stowage brackets for a hand crank and a tire pump on the interior of the lid, and the presence of the swirl air filter (Wirbelluftfilter) with its distinctive inverted-V appearance to the left side of the engine. (Randy Smith)

As seen in this left-side view of the very-late-production Type 82 Kübelwagen, except for subtle changes, the bodies of these vehicles underwent only minor changes during their 1940-1945 production: things such as changes in the door handles, the spare-tire spider, the horizontal reinforcements in the body, and the door hinges. (Randy Smith)

Kfz. 1
Leergew   0.76 t

Nutzlast   0.45 t
/e. Kl.   II

Schwimmwagen

General der Panzertruppe Maximilian von Edelsheim and his party leave in their Type 128 amphibious car for the east side of the Elbe river to convey the terms of surrender to their subordinate commanders. They have just left the city hall of Stendal, Germany on 4 May 1945, where staff of the 9th U.S. Army gave them the terms for the German XXXXVIII Panzer Corps of which Edelsheim commanded at the time. With only 30 Type 128s ever produced in 1941, this vehicle is certainly a rarity in 1945. It is in remarkably good condition, as well. It bears the markings of the XXXXVIII Panzer Corps on its right side and is painted with the standard three-tone paint scheme. (NARA)

Its markedly longer body tub can identify the Type 128. In addition, there are two distinct rounded handles mounted on the body near the top edge to assist in entering and exiting the vehicle. This is one of the early deliveries to the SS in 1941. It carries the very low license number of 384. (NARA)

Type 166 prototype number one is presented to Hitler on 20 August 1941. The Schwimmwagen prototype has several unique features not adopted on production vehicles. One of these features can be seen just under the left arm of the figure in the right foreground. A large cutout was created in front of the passenger to allow the gunner to more easily feed and operate the forward mounted MG 34. (NARA)

From this angle the lack of an indentation for the propeller is evident on the rear engine cover. The propeller has also not been installed on this example. The engine air intake mounted at the top is from a Type 128. Production Schwimmwagens mounted only a tail-light on the left fender, while this vehicle mounts one on each rear fender. Note the "166/1" stencil on the engine cover. (NARA)

This final shot shows the smaller windshield to good advantage, as well as the large MG34 "cupola" visible just in front of Hitler. The driver's windshield is also visible in the previous shot, along with the smaller dashboard. Unlike production vehicles, the Schwimmwagen prototype mounted Continental balloon tires. Headlights are mounted on brackets attached to the front bodywork, as opposed to the fenders of later Schwimmwagens. (NARA)

A Fallschirmjäger (paratrooper) maneuvers a Schwimmwagen that is painted overall in a dark color. On the deck to the rear of the rear seats are the muffler and the muffler shield. Stored above the muffler is a rod for raising and lowering the propeller. (BA 304-0635-37)

A Waffen-SS Schwimmwagen, license plate number SS-303865, is parked along a river. Attached to the marine propeller and leaning on the muffler shield is the rod for raising and lowering the propeller. The rod has a circular handle on the upper end. (NARA)

Reichsmarschall Hermann Göring (back to the camera) greets an SS officer in the courtyard Karinhall, Göring's private manor in Berlin, during World War II. The officer has just arrived in the Schwimmwagen, SS license number 302061. (BA 146-1979-175-10)

Three Schwimmwagens are in the foreground in a photo of a parade of men and vehicles of SS-Liebstandarte SS Adolf Hitler in Paris in August 1942. On the sides of their bodies are the tactical symbol for a Kradzug: motorcycle platoon. (BA 256-1228-10)

A Schwimmwagen negotiates a muddy street in a town in southern Ukraine during the first two months of 1944. With the rather skimpy fenders, mud has been splattered over much of the side of the body as well as on the front end of the vehicle. (BA 709-0347-15)

Two members of the Waffen-SS, proudly pose with their Schwimmwagen . The vehicle has a mottled, sprayed camouflage scheme over the base color. The tires are the narrow type. On the center of the bow is a swiveling tow hook. The full license plate number can be seen: SS-303669. Blackout covers are fitted over the headlights; these were of fabric construction with a slot on the front. (NARA)

Wehrmacht troops, including two wielding Sturmgewehr 44 (StG 44) assault rifles, are on the alert in a Schwimmwagen. Below the mirror is a stencil with information for shipping by rail, and the headlight partially covers a stencil giving the vehicle length, 3.83 meters. (BA 183-J28132)

In a photo likely related to the preceding one, troops cross a river in Schwimmwagens. On the closer vehicle, the hold-down clamps that secure the windshield in its lowered position are visible; these had spring catches and rubber bumpers. Of interest here is the pad on the vehicle sill just to the left of the driver's elbow. (BA 183-J28133)

Two soldiers use a Schwimmwagen to navigate a harbor area, perhaps during the crossing of the Seine in the summer of 1944. On the side of the body is a stencil with vehicular identification and weight data for railroad-shipment purposes, such as empty weight, load capacity, and freight classification. (NARA)

Elements of the Wehrmacht's 278th Infantry Division move into positions just prior to their surrender to the U.S. 14th Armored Division on 2 May 1945. The Schwimmwagen in the foreground is in excellent condition. It mounts tires with the heavier cross-country tread. The divisional insignia, a Hessian solder standing at ease, can be seen clearly on the VW and the BMW R75 behind it. (NARA)

The Volkswagen Type 166 Schwimmwagen was an all-wheel-drive amphibious vehicle that shared the same engine and certain other mechanical components as the Kübelwagen. Beyond that, the Schwimmwagen was a much different design. The Type 166 Schwimmwagen had a more rounded body than the Kübelwagen and a wheelbase that was 1.3 feet shorter. Shown here is a September 1943 model, body number 5273, with the insignia of the 1st SS-Panzer Division Liebstandarte-SS Adolf Hitler. Although the Model 166 was the most-produced amphibious car to date, with 15,584 manufactured, by all accounts its users appreciated the mobility afforded by its all-wheel drive more than its ability to cross bodies of water. (John Adams-Graf)

Top left: The body of the Schwimmwagen essentially formed a boat. It was watertight, of welded steel construction and monocoque design: that is, the skin provides the principal structural support. Internal cross braces added extra strength to the vehicle. (Rick Forys) **Top right:** A spare tire is secured to a recessed holder on the front deck of this early-1943-production Schwimmwagen. This type of tire was referred to as the "wide" type and was size 200-16. Narrow tires sometimes were used on the Schwimmwagen but provided less flotation.

Above left: On each front fender or mudguard, a large, three-piece service headlight was installed; these are the large, early type. To the lower right are several of the welded seams of the body. **Above right:** Two fuel filler necks and caps are on the front deck; these are connected to two fuel tanks below the deck. Stamped in raised figures to the front of the filler is "25L," referring to the capacity of each tank, 25 liters. To the rear of the filler is the right windshield clamp.

Top left: A service headlight is on the left fender. A tubular guard is welded to the front of the body and fastened to the fenders. Also in view is the filler and cap for the left fuel tank.
Top right: Details of the Continental 200-16 wide spare tire, its tread pattern, and the design of the wheel rim are in view. Although the spare tire carrier is not visible in the recess on the deck, it consists of a drum-shaped holder with four arms to spread the weight. **Above left:** The left fuel filler and cap are in the foreground; "25L" is stamped in raised figures to the

front of the filler, as on the right side of the front deck. Beyond the fuel filler is a smaller filler neck and cap for the central lubrication tank, which supplies oil to the front axle. **Above right:** The left steering rack is viewed from the front. As on the Kübelwagen, transverse torsion bars are present, but the Schwimmwagen adds half-shafts connected to a differential. A large, hardened-steel protection pan is bolted to the lower part of the bow.

A restored October 1943-production Schwimmwagen, body number 6230, exhibits a Dunkelgelb (dark yellow) paint scheme. Stowed on the left side of the body are a shovel and a wooden paddle. A tubular bumper along the side of the body is attached to the front and rear fenders. A weight and classification stencil is on the side of the body. To the right side of the vehicle in front of the front passenger's seat is a MG 34 machine gun mount. Other elements in view include the muffler above the rear deck and the raised water propeller at the rear of the vehicle.

Kfz. K2s
Leergew 0.8
Nutzlast 0.45 t
Ve. Kl   II

1.8 atü

2.2 atü

Top left: A feature of 1942-43 production Schwimmwagens is a rounded upper inner corner on each side of the windshield. Later in production, this was changed to a right-angle corner to simplify the production of the windshield frame and the cutting of the windshield glass.
Top right: The windshield was usually lowered and secured in the two clips when the Schwimmwagen was being operated on water. A locking wing nut is on each side of the windshield. Next to the windshield is the mounting socket for a machine gun. **Above left:** In the cab, above the steering column is a shifting diagram. To the right of the column is the fuel cock. Above the speedometer on the instrument panel is the fuse box. Above the steering wheel is the windshield-wiper motor; only one motor was present. **Above right:** The steering wheel has three metal spokes; on the hub is the horn button. Resting in a holder on the rear face of the bin in the center background is a small oilcan. Partially visible above the can is the socket-insertable-type jack in the stowed position.

Elements of the cab are observed from the left side of an October 1943 Schwimmwagen. On the left windshield bracket is the rear-view mirror. The windshield motor on the bottom of the windshield frame is powered by the electrical cable that passes from the top of the instrument panel. On the tunnel between the front seats are the transmission shift lever and the parking brake lever. Under the dash to the right of the instrument panel is a toolbox in a clamp-type holder.

As on the Kübelwagen, wooden decking is on the floor of the Schwimmwagen. The V-shaped fitting to the right of the instrument panel is the holder for the metal toolbox, unfastened and swung down on its hinges. To the right are ammunition drums for an MG 34. (John Adams-Graf)

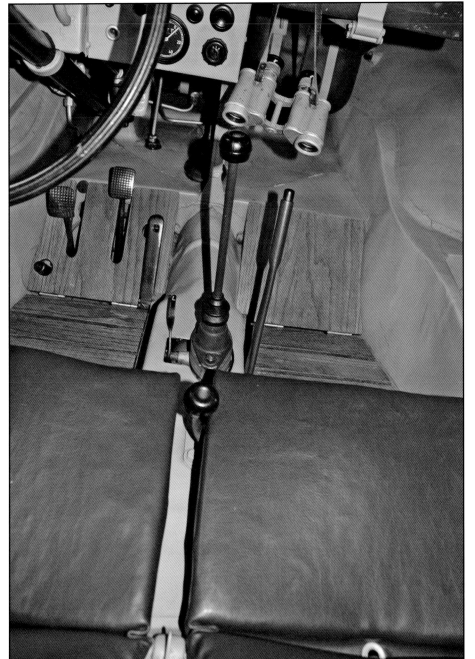

Left: In a view of the cab from between the front seats, on the panel below the steering column are the headlight dimmer footswitch, the clutch pedal, brake pedal, and accelerator pedal. The knob between the seats is at the top of the front-wheel-drive shift lever. Immediately to the left of the base of the transmission shift lever on the tunnel is an operating lever for the carburetor choke control. A pair of binoculars hangs above the transmission shift lever and the parking brake lever. **Top right:** From left to right, as viewed over the driver's seat, are the carburetor choke (marked with a white "L" on the end), the parking brake lever, the transmission shift lever and the front-wheel-drive shift lever. In the right background is a Jerrycan marked for holding water. **Above right:** As viewed from the front right seat, to the left is the lowered holder for the metal toolbox. At the center is a rack with ammunition drums, above which is the folding travel lock for the machine gun. The base of the pedestal for the machine gun is attached to the wheel well. (John Adams-Graf, all)

The front and rear bucket seats were of a much sleeker design than the seats of the Kübelwagen. Behind the front seats is a crossbar that added structural strength to the body. To the left is a case for spare MG 34 barrels. To the rear is the folded top. (John Adams-Graf)

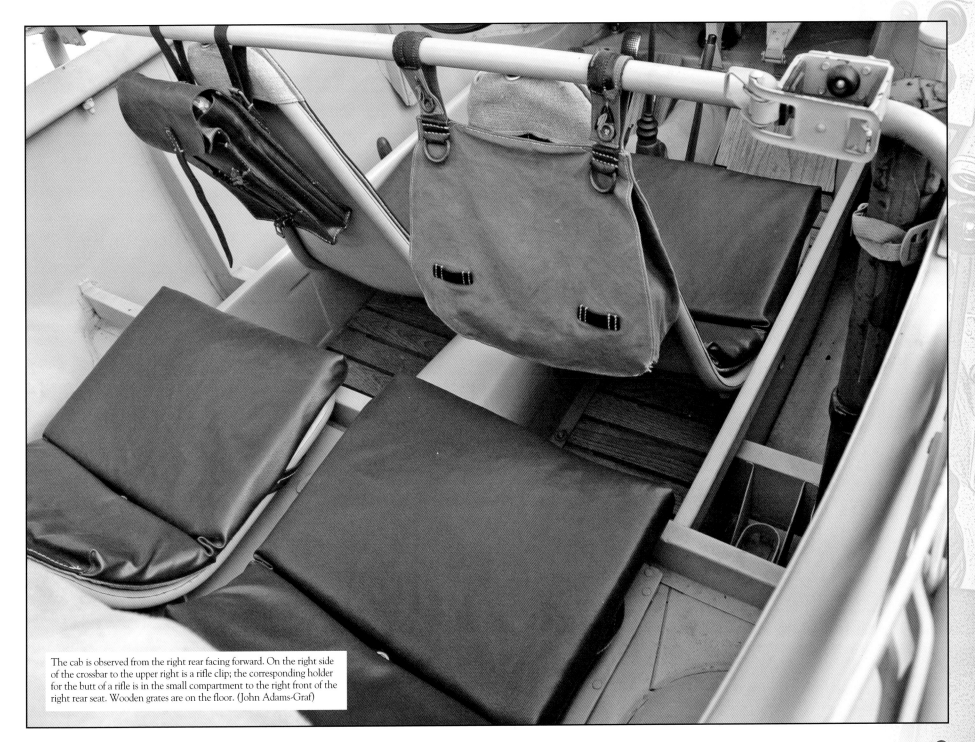

The cab is observed from the right rear facing forward. On the right side of the crossbar to the upper right is a rifle clip; the corresponding holder for the butt of a rifle is in the small compartment to the right front of the right rear seat. Wooden grates are on the floor. (John Adams-Graf)

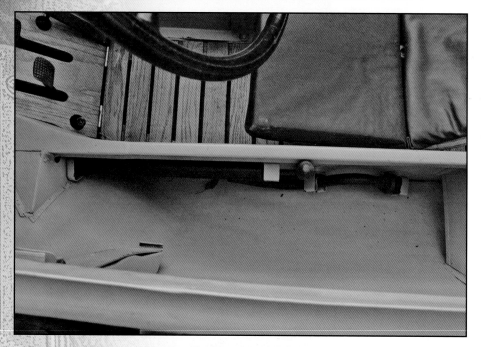

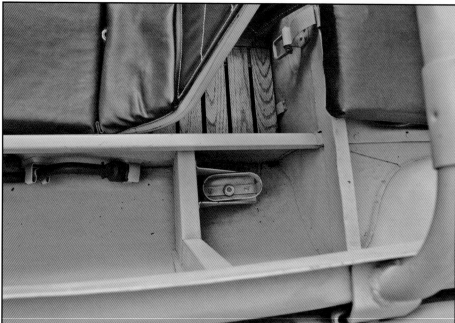

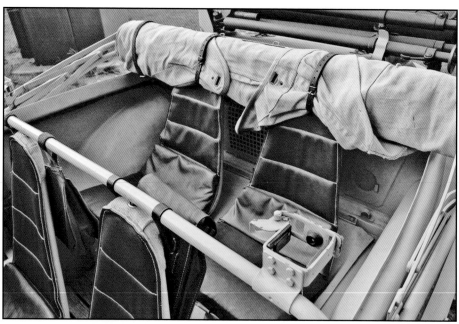

Top left: A low bulkhead runs fore and aft to the outboard sides of the seats. This one runs alongside the driver's seat. The bulkhead forms an open compartment between the seats and the body, where the manual hand crank for starting the engine as well as an air pump were to be stowed. To the lower right is a cross-frame. **Top right:** In a view extending to the rear of the preceding one, the part of the low bulkhead alongside the left rear passenger's seat is shown. In the small compartment at the center is a holder for the butt of a stowed rifle; to the right is part of the upper holder for the rifle. **Above left:** Stowed adjacent to the right seat are two cases for spare barrels for an MG 34; the one to the left held two gun barrels, while the darker one to the right held a single barrel. Above the ammunition drums to the right is the travel lock for the MG 34, folded down. **Above right:** The seat cushions came in several different materials. They were held in place with a pocket at the top that fit over the top of the seat shell, and two straps on the lower front corners that slipped over the shell. The left rifle clip is in the foreground. (John Adams-Graf, all)

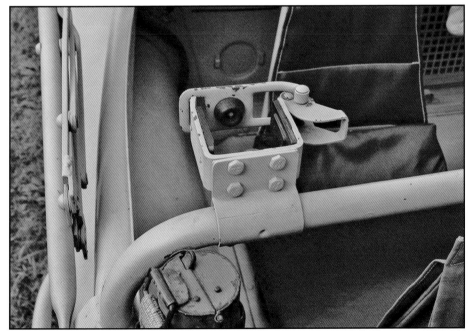

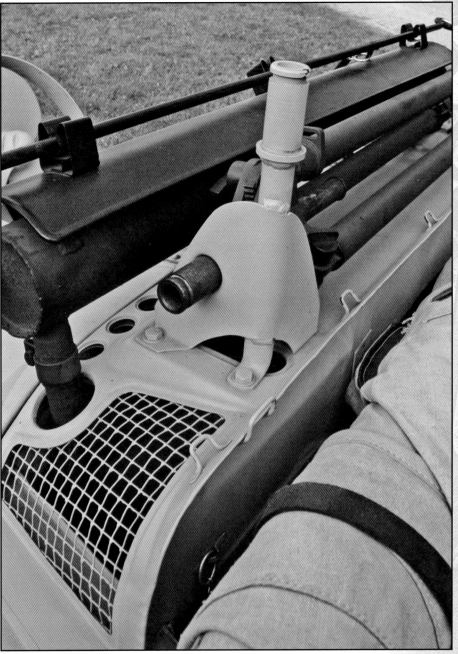

Top left: To the rear of the rear seats is the folded convertible top, secured with leather or canvas straps. Above the top, an antiaircraft machine gun tripod is strapped to the front of the muffler. The vertical tube to the left is the rear pedestal mount for a machine gun. **Right:** The rear machine gun pedestal is observed from the right side of the Schwimmwagen. The tubular pedestal is reinforced with a bent-steel brace. A hole in the brace acts as a holder for the top of the antiaircraft machine gun tripod when it is stowed. **Above Left:** The right rifle clip is observed close-up from the front, with the front passenger's seat to the lower right. Note the rubber bumpers on the inner sides of the clip. Hot air is exhausted from the engine compartment through the screen at left bottom of this image. (John Adams-Graf, all)

Top left: The left rifle clip is being put to use as a holder for a "potato-masher" hand grenade and as a post from which to hang a Stahlhelm with Waffen-SS markings. Details of the frame for the convertible top and its manner of attachment to the body are also in view. **Top right:** In a view of the left rear side of a September 1943 Schwimmwagen, the recommended tire pressure, 2.2 atü, is stenciled on the fender. Above the paddle is the left side of the muffler and a ventilation grille. To the rear of the vehicle is the raised water propeller. **Above left:** To the outboard side of the bracket for the left taillight is a crescent-shaped holder for the paddle. Above the paddle, the exhaust pipe passes up through a round opening in the rear deck to the muffler. The muffler and exhaust was raised to protect the engine from water. **Above right:** The paddle holder and taillight bracket are viewed from the front. Above the taillight is the exhaust tail pipe. The three pointed bases of the antiaircraft machine gun tripod are at the upper center. To the rear of the grille is one of the latches for the engine-access lid. (John Adams-Graf, all)

With the lid open, the engine compartment is displayed. The KdF 1131 cc engine was the same used in the Kübelwagen from chassis number 17001 in March 1943. To the left is the carburetor air intake; the oil-bath air cleaner is at the center with the red label. (John Adams-Graf)

To the front of the engine is the cooling-fan enclosure. To the upper right is a green container for the cold weather starting valve to mix fuel and ether for the engine in extreme cold. The aluminum-colored mechanism at the center is the carburetor, to the lower left of which is the distributor. (John Adams-Graf)

The engine-compartment lid has a rubber waterproofing seal around its inner perimeter. To the right is a hold-open arm. At the upper center of the bulkhead at the front of the engine compartment is the manufacturer's plate. Several of the lid latches are visible.

When not in use for operating in water, the propeller assembly was swung upward and secured with a strap in this position. The power shaft for the propeller is at the lower rear of the body. The rod stowed atop the muffler was for lowering and raising the propeller. Schwimmwagen propeller drive assemblies were made of steel and aluminum castings during 1942-43, but during 1944 these components became stamped sheet metal. Two tailpipes exit the muffler on 1943 Schwimmwagens like this one. In 1944 only a single tailpipe, exiting the right side of the muffler, was used. (John Adams-Graf)

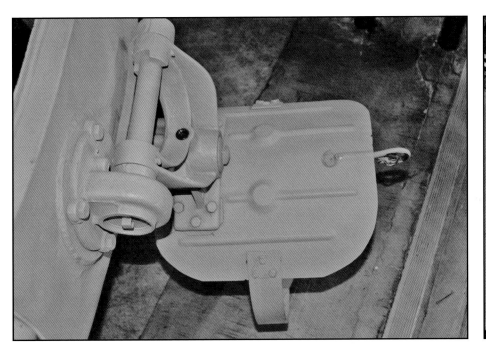

Top left: The propeller assembly of an early-1943 Schwimmwagen is in the lowered position. When in that position, the propeller receives power from the engine by means of engaging a dog clutch. The propeller assembly is on a sprung, hinged mounting. (John Adams-Graf) **Top right:** The propeller assembly is raised, showing the toothed dog clutch situated in the diamond-shaped plate at the bottom center of the rear of the body. The propeller is raised and lowered by means of a rod attached to the hook on the top rear of the propeller hood. **Above**

left: The pivoting mounting on the rear of the body of the Schwimmwagen that supports the water-propeller assembly is viewed close-up from the left side. A detailed view is also offered of an engine-compartment lid latch, with a lever and a bent-wire catch. **Above right:** The propeller assembly is viewed from below in its raised position. The propeller is connected to a case containing a chain drive, on the bottom of which is a metal skid. The bottom of the ring-shaped guard for the propeller is attached to the bottom of the skid.

Top left: This is what the rear of the propeller looks like in the raised position. A webbing strap attached to a loop fastened to the engine-compartment lid serves to hold the propeller assembly in the "up" position. The hood and ring-shaped guard are also in view. **Top right:** Further details of the design of the skid on the bottom of the housing, which also serves to support the bottom of the ring guard, are available from this angle. The dog clutch is at the bottom center. To each side of the rear of the body is a tow hook on a swivel mount. **Above left:** The retainer strap for the propeller assembly is attached to a loop welded at an angle on the right side of the guard ring of the propeller. The hook that projects from the hood is used along with a detachable rod to raise and lower the entire propeller assembly. **Above right:** The rear of the Schwimmwagen is viewed, with part of the propeller assembly at the bottom and the muffler at the top. A retainer cord is attached to the engine-compartment lid and to the rod for raising and lowering the propeller, stowed on the muffler. (John Adams-Graf)

Top left: As observed from the right side, a muffler guard is mounted over the muffler, and the rod for raising and lowering the propeller is stowed on brackets atop this guard. A tailpipe is on each side of the Schwimmwagen muffler. Also in view is the rear machine gun mount. (John Adams-Graf) **Top right:** Each of the rear tow hooks on this early-1943 Schwimmwagen is on a swivel mount at the rear end of two hat-channel reinforcing ribs that are the shape of an inclined V. (Rick Forys) **Above left:** The grilles on each side of the rear deck and the grille between the rear seats on the rear bulkhead of the crew compartment exhaust cooling air from the engine compartment. Footman-type loops are fastened to the upper part of the body for securing the canvas top when it is raised. **Above right:** Details of the crossbar behind the front seats and of the frame for the convertible top are observed from the right side. Of tubular steel construction, the crossbar served to lend structural strength to the body and also provided a place to locate the two rifle clips. (John Adams-Graf, last two)

Top left: An MG 34 is installed on the forward gun mount. The travel lock is in the raised position and is attached to the lower rear of the receiver. To fire the machine gun, the travel lock was disengaged and lowered, enabling the gunner to freely swing and aim the weapon. **Top right:** The upper part of the travel lock for the MG 34 is seen from the right side. **Above left:** The pintle-type cradle of the MG 34 as mounted on an early-1943 Schwimmwagen is viewed from the right side. The machine gun is also equipped with a standard bipod, shown in the folded position, for firing the gun from a prone position on the ground when desired. **Above right:** A 1943 Schwimmwagen is observed from the right front. Beneath the front fender is a bent tube that served both as a brace for the fender and a headlight wiring conduit. To the far right is the front tow hook in a recess in the bow. Midway along the bumper that stretches between the front and the rear fenders is a bumper support bracket. Extending slightly from the lower part of the body to the front of the rear wheel is a tube for inserting the jack.

A restored 1943 production Schwimmwagen is displayed. This vehicle retains several features in common with the early Schwimmwagen, including the horn on the front right of the body, the narrow fenders with tubular bumpers spanning the space between the front and the rear fenders, and the rounded inner upper corners of the windshield. The horn remains on the right front of the body to the front of the fender. The original-type 160mm headlights were not available when this vehicle was restored, and smaller headlights were fitted as shown here.

Schwimmwagen (Type 166)

Length	3.825 meters
Width	1.48 meters
Height	1.615 meters top up, 1.080 top down
Weight	1,362 kgs
Fuel capacity	50 liters
Maximum Speed	80 km/hr land, 10 km/hr on water
Range, on road	520 km
Engine make	Volkswagen
Engine configuration	4-cylinder, horizontally opposed, air-cooled
Engine displacement	1131 cc
Engine horsepower	25 @3000 RPM

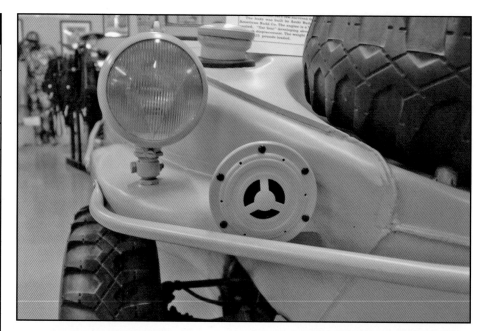

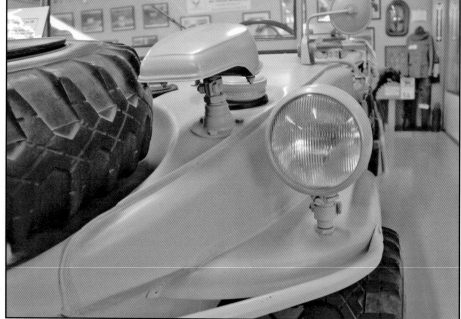

Top right: The right service headlight and the horn on a mid-production Schwimmwagen are viewed from the front. Also in view are several of the raised seams of the bodywork and the right side of the tubular bumper, including its attachment point on the left front fender.
Above left: A Continental spare tire and wheel assembly is secured to its carrier on the front of the Schwimmwagen. Note the small tie-down loop fastened to the rear inner surface of the tire carrier. A Notek blackout headlight is now mounted on the left side of the spare tire.
Above right: The Notek blackout headlight, a field modification, was used when service headlights could disclose a vehicle's presence to the enemy, emitted a diffuse light that enabled the driver to see the road but could not be seen from above or the sides or from the front at any significant distance.

In the foreground, in a recess on the left side of the front deck, is the filler and cap for the left fuel tank, with "25L" stamped in raised figures to the front. Beyond this filler is the filler for the central lubrication system. Between the fillers is the left windshield clamp.

The front of the cab of a mid-production Schwimmwagen is displayed. The instrument panel has a speedometer, a switch for illuminating the speedometer, a red charging indicator, a green oil indicator lamp, and a combination light and ignition switch.

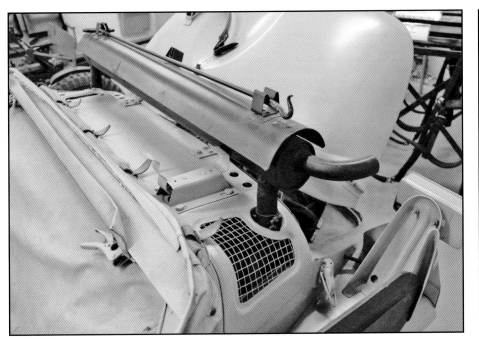

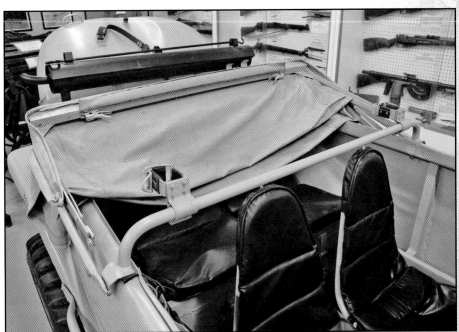

Top left: To the rear of the crew compartment is the muffler with a shield on top. Mounted on the deck inboard of the ventilation grille is a clamp-type holder for an antiaircraft machine-gun tripod. To the right are holders for the Notek blackout taillight and a boat paddle. **Top right:** A Schwimmwagen is shown with the antiaircraft machine-gun tripod secured on the rear deck. Fastened to clips on top of the muffler shield is the rod used by a crewman to raise and lower the water propeller. The propeller is raised, to the far right. **Above left:** The lid is open, revealing the engine compartment. The features are similar to those in the early-production Schwimmwagen, with the carburetor-air ducts and air cleaner prominent from this angle. To the left above the registration plate is the Notek blackout taillight. **Above right:** Features visible on this 1943 Schwimmwagen include the crossbar behind the front seats with two rifle clips attached, the vertical rib on the right side of the body, the collapsed convertible top and frame, and the muffler assembly above the rear deck.

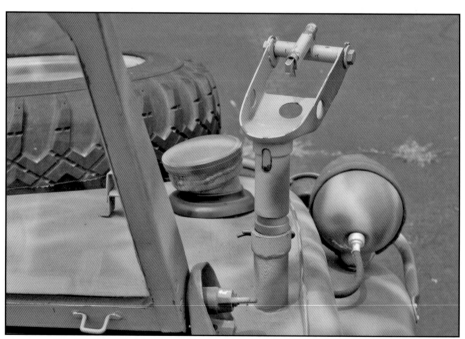

Top left: Details of the right side of the frame for the convertible top are displayed. The top and frame for the Schwimmwagen were of a completely different design than those of the Kübelwagen and involved one central support bow that pivoted at the point shown here. **Top right:** Underneath the dash to the left is the toolbox. To the right is the travel lock for the machine gun, in the stowed position. To secure the gun in the travel position, at the top of the lock are two sprung toggles with holes that engage pins to the rear of the gun grip. **Above left:** The travel lock for the machine gun is viewed from above. The two toggles and their coil springs are visible to the front (top) of the travel lock. Squeezing the bottoms of the toggles causes their tops to spread so the lock can be engaged or disengaged. **Above right:** The forward machine gun mount is viewed from the rear; the pintle-type cradle is swung to the rear. To the front of the mount are the filler and filler cap for the right fuel tank. To the right is the rear of the 1944 right service headlight, including its electrical cable. The wiring exited the rear of the 130mm headlights, as here, rather than through the bottom, as was the case with the 160mm headlights.

This restored vehicle, owned by Bob Graebe, painted in Dunkelgelb with sprayed camouflage of green is an example of a Schwimmwagen from the July 1944 production run. This vehicle has body number 7-013598. The dark-colored wheel rims contrast prominently against the Dunkelgelb wheel hubs. The previously-used fender support, which also contained the headlight wiring for 160mm headlights, was discontinued in 1944 when the 130mm headlights were introduced.

SS - 929301

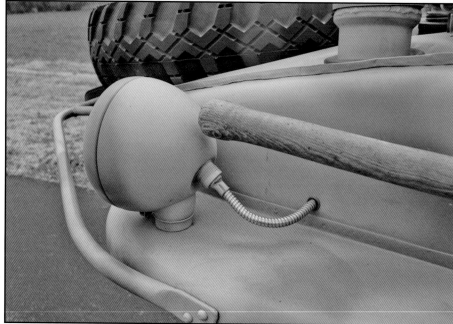

SS
929301

Top left: The spare tire and its carrier are viewed from the front. **Top right:** The left service headlight is displayed. A flexible metal conduit conveys the electrical cable to the unit. The end of the front bumper or grab bar is fastened to the front fender with two large rivets. Also in view are a wooden shovel handle and the left fuel filler and cap. **Above left:** The left rear of the side of a July 1944 Schwimmwagen is in view, offering a clear view of the clip for the paddle handle. Stretching between the front and the rear fenders, in addition to the tubular bumper, is a piece of steel channel attached to the body. The 1944 muffler with single tailpipe is present. Near the center bottom of the muffler a small tube is visible, extending into the engine compartment, where it will join the new Wirbellufifilter air cleaner, introduced on the 1944 Schwimmwagens and 1943 Kübelwagens. **Above right:** A service taillight is mounted on the bracket on the left fender of this Schwimmwagen. Below it is a reproduction Waffen-SS registration plate. The reinforcing channels for the rear tow hook in the shape of an inclined V are clearly visible from this angle.

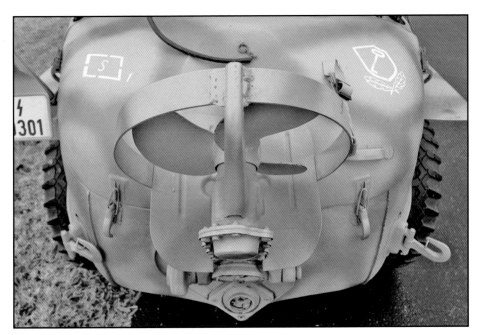

Top left: In a view of the rear of a July 1944 Schwimmwagen, the propeller assembly is in the raised position for operation on land. The propeller drive housing used in 1944 was made of stamped sheet metal, as here, in contrast to the previously used cast drive housing. Toward the top center is the retainer for the propeller-lowering and –raising rod stowed on top of the muffler shield. **Top right:** The rear machine gun mount is viewed from the front. The hole in the bent steel reinforcing bracket at the bottom of the mount was for holding the top of an antiaircraft machine-gun tripod. Details of the muffler, shield, and propeller rod are available.

Above left: In the 1944 version of the engine compartment, the oil-bath filter is no longer present, having been replaced by the Wirbelluffilter, and the carburetor-air duct has been rerouted to the upper center of the bulkhead. To the right of the carburetor is the ether tank for starting the engine in extreme cold temperatures. **Above right:** The rear seats of a 1944 Schwimmwagen have been removed, allowing an unobstructed view of the rear bulkhead of the crew compartment. At the center is the cooling-air intake for the engine. The stencils on each side translate to "do not cover."

The Kübelwagen and, as seen here, its amphibious, all-wheel drive sibling, the Schwimmwagen, provided the Wehrmacht and the Waffen-SS with two very useful, smaller vehicles in World War II. Used in the wide range of geographic areas Nazi Germany was involved in, under a variety of climatic extremes, these two vehicles shuttled personnel, performed in scouting and reconnaissance roles, and served as utility and special-purpose vehicles. A number of restored surviving vehicles continue to delight enthusiasts and spectators seven decades after they were produced.